Christina Toll

Musings © 2022 Christina Toll

All rights reserved.

No part of this publication may be reproduced, stored in a retrieval system, or transmitted, in any form or by any means, electronic, mechanical, photocopying, recording or otherwise, without the prior written permission of the presenters.

Christina Toll asserts the moral right to be identified as author of this work.

Presentation by *BookLeaf Publishing*

Web: www.bookleafpub.com

E-mail: info@bookleafpub.com

ISBN: 9789357615853

First edition 2022

Zachary

The day you were born
Unadulterated joy
Love you forever.

Sean

I wasn't expecting to love you.
Disappointment was all I'd known before.
Thought I'd never find my true soulmate.
But then you showed up at my door.

Your smile I felt deep in my bones.
The spark between us was intense.
It was like I'd known you forever.
Although it didn't really make sense.

You are the sweetest man in the world.
Unafraid to show how much you care.
I've never once had a doubt how you feel about me.
And to you my soul I've laid bare.

MMFA

Cool popsicles and hot kisses.
We talked for hours during that first visit.
You stole my heart, but I don't miss it.
Because you've made me whole in so many ways.
And I'm going to love you until the end of my days.

Music

There is nothing like a song
To make you feel like you belong
In a world full of hate
That you can't connect to or relate
Music fills the void lifelong.

Water

I am water, flowing and deep
In the cold, wet depths my secrets do keep.
I adapt and am strong, dependent on need
Calm and restrained or raging when freed.

I am water, fluid and clean
Removing the bad so the good can be seen.
A warm, wet embrace, soothing and loving
Refreshingly honest and sometimes
soul-crushing.

Books

Books are magical things.
They take you to places you've never been.
Introduce you to people you've never met.
Give you things you'd never normally get.

Books are a perfect escape.
From the tediousness of the day-to-day.
From a job at which you aren't skilled.
From a life that leaves you unfulfilled.

Books are good for your mind.
They are insightful and help you unwind.
Feed your imagination and boost your IQ.
Cheer you up when you're feeling blue.

Books are a wonderful gift.
To be used as you see fit.
For entertainment or to learn.
Beneficial their pages are to turn.

Baseball

The mechanics of a pitch
The speed of the ball
The cheers of the crowd
The umpire's call.

The crack of the bat
The heat of the sun
The crunch of the dirt
The thrill of a run.

The swing and a miss
The throw a bit wild
The count is at full
The last pitch outside.

The thrill of a late-inning rally
The agony of just falling short
The emotions evoked like a rollercoaster
The beauty of this perfect sport.

Ottawa

My hometown, the city I love.
Beautiful in all four seasons
Regardless of weather.

My hometown, the city I love.
So much to explore
History, arts and culture.

My hometown, the city I love.
Surrounded by water and green space
It is breathtaking.

My hometown, the city I love.
Honouring our heritage and identity
Through celebrations and festivals.

My hometown, the city I love.
No matter how far I go
Ottawa will always be home.

Architects

Everyone who knows me,
Knows how much I love my parents.
Everyone who knows them, knows why.
They are my architects.

Every bit of goodness in me
Is because of the example they set.
Every bit of love in me
Is because of the strength of theirs.

Blessed beyond measure am I
Being raised by these amazing humans.
Individually and as a couple
They are what we all should aspire to be.

Sister

My very first friend
You've been with me through it all
I am so grateful.

Ecdysis

Young and naive
Too light for that dark
It slowly consumed and
Extinguished the spark.

Lived in the depths
Like a snake, blood turned cold
Waiting it out
Life put on hold.

Sacrifices made
Self-preservation the goal
Heartbeat a murmur
On ice was the soul.

Then the dark fled
Thinking no good remained
But it was still there
Just in hiding, restrained.

Away from the dark
Warmth and feeling returned
Old life, like skin, shed
Past behaviours unlearned.

Never again
Will the dark be allowed
To step into the light
That is avowed.

The Domain

Four girls looking to make a splash
Worked at the Biway for cash
They cashiered and folded
And sometimes were scolded
But together always had a blast!

New Orleans

You called to me
With the promise of adventure
And I answered.

You embraced me
With your humid heat
And I came alive.

You serenaded me
With your musical genius
And I danced.

You tantalized me
With your culinary prowess
And I was revived.

You dazzled me
With your Creole grace
And I was awestruck.

You marked me
Deep in my soul
And I am forever changed.

Motherhood

All your hopes and dreams,
Wrapped up in another human being.
Motherhood

The deepest love of your life,
And the greatest cause of your strife.
Motherhood

The most fulfilling role,
Although it takes its toll.
Motherhood

The source of endless pride,
An unforgettable ride.
Motherhood

Patience

It takes time to build a forever
If it's easy it likely won't last
Life is a series of twists and turns
Take it slow rather than going fast.

A virtue they say patience is
I simply say it's a must
It takes time to build solid foundations,
And to be sure of who it is you can trust.

Captures

Take a photo, draw a picture,
Film a video, utter a word.
All moments in time.
Sights seen and sounds heard.
Quickly gone, but preserved.

Altruism

A simple smile
A helping hand
A sweet hello
A gesture grand.

A token gift
A word of praise
A listening ear
An appreciative gaze.

Kindness is
Just being there
Doing anything
To show you care.

Anthophile

Every flower has a story.
A symbol of idealism
In a too-realistic world.

Every flower has strength.
Growing through the dirt
To bloom and unfurl.

Every flower has beauty.
A buffet for the senses
In smell, feel and sight.

Every flower has hope.
To grow strong and
Stand tall in the sunlight.

Motivation

Holding fast
To the past
Even though
You already know
It no longer serves you.
Don't do it.

Move on
When the line is drawn
Be brave
Do not waive
Your right to happiness.
Just do it.

Brightside

It's taken a lifetime
To feel comfortable in my skin.
Content with who I am
And at ease with where I've been.

I have wrinkles and scars
Failures and baggage.
But I've learned from it all
Despite all the damage.

I'm at peace with my past
And all that I've done.
What I'm evolving into
And the person I've become.

No fear or shame
You get what you see.
I am what I am
Imperfectly me.

Happiness

A comforting hug
The smell of warm bread
My favourite song
A freshly made bed.

The first sip of coffee
A really great book
Sea salt and toffee
Not having to cook.

A job well done
The thrill of success
Finding "the one"
A loving caress.

Family celebrations
Good times with friends
Adventurous vacations
Relaxing weekends.

A goodnight text or call
The joy of giving
Things big and small
That make life worth living.

Printed in the USA
CPSIA information can be obtained
at www.ICGtesting.com
LVHW021052141123
763890LV00003B/299